THIRD
ASSESSMENT P...

ENGLISH

ANSWER BOOK

JM BOND

Nelson

Paper 1

Underline the right answers.

In its first form, raffia work was simply the interlacing of grasses and rushes, and this was being done many thousands of years ago.

Raffia is a kind of palm tree that grows on the islands round Madagascar. The leaves of this tree grow to nearly fifteen metres in length. The material we know as raffia comes from these leaves. The inner skins of the leaves are peeled and then stretched out in the tropical sun, which dries and bleaches them. The dried raffia is made up into hanks, and sold by weight. Natural raffia is a creamy colour but it can be dyed very easily. If you find the raffia stiff to handle you can soak it for an hour or two in water, and leave it to dry. Raffia can be plaited, twisted, woven, knotted, stitched and embroidered.

1   This passage could be called (Madagascar, Raffia, Crafts)

2   Raffia is made from (palm leaves, rushes, grasses, plaits)

3   To bleach is (to sand, to colour, to wet, to whiten)

4   Which part of the leaf is used to make raffia?
    (The inside, the peel, the outside)

5   How can you soften raffia?
    (By peeling it, by bleaching it, by wetting it)

6–7   Before raffia was used, which two things did the first people use?
      (Plaits, palms, hanks, grasses, rushes)

8   Hanks are (handkerchiefs, loops or coils, weights)

9   Leaves of the raffia palm are (wide, stretched, pointed, long, round)

10–15 Can you arrange the letters in heavy type to form words?

We had a lovely **prupes** ....supper.... last night. Mum cooked some

hfsi ....fish.... and chips and some **seap** ....peas.... Then we had

an **plepa** ....apple.... crumble and cream. I was still hungry so I had

some biscuits, **ttubre** ....butter.... and **hsceee** ....cheese....

Fill in the following group names.

16 A ....flock.... of sheep   17 A ....hive or swarm.... of bees

18 A ....troop.... of monkeys   19 A ....flock.... of birds

20 A ....litter.... of puppies   21 A ....shoal.... of fish

22 A ....gaggle.... of geese   23 A ....herd.... of cattle

In each of the following lines underline the word that means the same as the word on the left.

24 **often**   seldom   always   frequently   never   sometimes

25 **conceal** hide   stick   show   confess   confide

26 **repair**   break   repast   remain   make   mend

27 **abandon** bandage   leave   collect   lose   find

28 **remote**   surrounding   near   mean   distant   close

Underline the nouns in this passage.

29–36 My aunt and uncle came to stay with us last Wednesday. Next week
we are taking them to the theatre to see a pantomime called "Puss in
Boots".

Fill in the following spaces with either **to**, **too** or **two**.

37 There are ....two.... girls here.

38 I will give it ....to.... him.

39 Steven said that Paul and his brother went ....too....

The name of an animal appears in each line. Write the name in the space.

40 You catch balls well. _____ cat

41 He scowled when he couldn't do it. _____ cow (or owl)

42 He had a red tassel on his cap. _____ ass

43 They trampled all over the garden. _____ ram

44 He threw everything on the floor. _____ ewe

45 "Where are you going to advertise it?" _____ toad

Where do the following live ?

46 pig _____ sty _____   47 vicar _____ vicarage _____   48 bird _____ nest _____

49 Eskimo _____ igloo _____   50 traveller _____ caravan _____   51 bee _____ hive _____

52 lion _____ den _____   53 nun _____ convent _____   54 monk _____ monastery _____

Put inverted commas (speech marks) in the following passage:

55–62 "I'm not coming back to school any more," said Anne.
       Diana gasped and stared at Anne to see if she meant it. "Will Marilla let you stay at home?" she asked.
       "She'll have to," said Anne. "I'll never go to school to that man again."
                          From *Anne of Green Gables* by L.M. Montgomery

Put these words in dictionary order.

flame   fire   flood   first   flap   flop

63 (1) _____ fire _____   64 (2) _____ first _____   65 (3) _____ flame _____

66 (4) _____ flap _____   67 (5) _____ flood _____   68 (6) _____ flop _____

69–74 Some words can be given an opposite meaning by putting the prefix **un** or **dis** in front of them. Can you put these words in the right column?

selfish   honest   agree   certain   order   common

un	dis
selfish	honest
certain	agree
common	order

4

In this short rhyme two words are missing. Can you fill them in?

75–76 Girls scream
Boys shout;
Dogs bark

School's ...out...
Cats run
Horses shy;
Into trees

Birds ...fly...

Complete the following adjectives of comparison.
Example: good   better   best

77–78	rich	richer	richest
79–80	bad	worse	worst
81–82	quiet	quieter	quietest
83–84	pretty	prettier	prettiest
85–86	many	more	most
87–88	early	earlier	earliest

Write the opposite of the word in heavy type.

89 The sea was very **rough.**   calm

90 She **bought** a book.   sold

91 It was a **dull** day.   bright

92 The dress was **beautiful.**   ugly

93 Karen **always** laughs.   never

94 Mum was very **sad.**   happy

Many things go together, such as **bucket and spade**. Complete the following.

95 Shoes and socks   96 Soap and water

97 Knife and fork   98 Needle and cotton/thread

99 Bread and butter   100 Hat and coat

Underline the right answers.

There is a lake near our town and it is very popular with both adults and children. Many boys and girls have their own sailing boats, which are called "Cadets". The grown-ups have many types of boats, but the most popular are the "Herons" and the "Enterprises". The Sailing Club is at the south end of the lake and at the opposite end is a boathouse where visitors can hire various craft – sailing boats, rowing boats and canoes. Towards the middle of the lake on one side there is a part which is roped off. This is used for swimming. Sometimes a sailing boat capsizes, and as the water is not very deep this can provide much merriment for the onlookers! There are many reasons why a boat may capsize. Usually it is caused by a violent gust of wind, but it may be due to overloading, a faulty boat, or simply lack of skill in handling the craft.

1–3 What kinds of boats are there on the lake?
(Sailing boats, steamers, rowing boats, canoes, cruisers)

4 What is at the south end of the lake?
(The Sailing Club, the boathouse, the swimming area)

5 What is in the middle?
(A place for swimming, the Sailing Club, the boathouse)

6 Name the sailing boats used by children. (Cadets, Herons, Enterprises)

7 If I wanted to hire a boat to which end should I go? (North, south)

8–9 Name the most popular sailing boats used by adults.
(Eagles, Herons, Mustangs, Fireflies, Enterprises, Cadets)

10–13 Underline the reasons why the boats capsize.
(There are too many boats, lack of skill, overloading, lack of paint, wind, rain, faulty boats)

14–19 Underline the verbs.

As he was late, the boy ran to the station. He hurried on to the platform and boarded the train a second or two before the guard waved his flag and the train moved away.

Look at each verb (doing word) on the left, and then see which of the words in the list on the right of the page best describes it.

20	arrived	punctually	carefully
21	waited	patiently	generously
22	slept	soundly	punctually
23	worked	carefully	patiently
24	gave	generously	soundly

Write one of these four prepositions in each space.

with   over   from   up

25 He ran ....up.... the stairs.

26 The teacher was cross ....with.... the cheeky boy.

27 Your T-shirt is different ....from.... mine.

28 The boy climbed ....over.... the wall.

Give the feminine of the following words.

29	actor	actress	**30**	hero	heroine
31	master	mistress	**32**	man	woman
33	uncle	aunt	**34**	nephew	niece
35	waiter	waitress	**36**	bull	cow

37 A young sheep is called a ......lamb......

38 A young lion is called a ......cub......

39 A young duck is called a ......duckling......

40 A young goose is called a ......gosling......

41 A young horse is called a ......foal......

42 A young cow is called a ......calf......

43 A young hen is called a ......chick......

44 A young goat is called a ......kid......

Fill in the following spaces with **past** or **passed**.

45 We went ....past.... the gate.

46 We ...passed... the cinema.

47 John ...passed... the book to his sister.

48 The cars flashed ....past....

49 I crept ....past.... the bedroom door.

50 Tom ...passed... the ball to the goalkeeper.

Underline the word which rhymes with the word on the left.

51	**come**	home	<u>drum</u>	foam	loam
52	**love**	wove	<u>dove</u>	tore	gave
53	**cow**	sew	low	<u>how</u>	mow
54	**guest**	host	worst	most	<u>quest</u>
55	**yolk**	silk	talk	<u>poke</u>	sulk

In each of the following lines there is a word which does not fit in with the rest. Underline that word.

56	glass	<u>table</u>	cup	plate	saucer
57	green	blue	yellow	<u>sky</u>	red
58	pen	pencil	chalk	crayon	<u>book</u>
59	dog	rabbit	<u>hutch</u>	mouse	cat

60	fish	pork	mutton	lamb	veal
61	leg	arm	foot	sock	hand
62	ring	watch	ear-ring	bracelet	ribbon
63	window	garden	door	roof	chimney

Write in full the words for which these abbreviations stand.

64	Jan	January
65	M.P.	Member of Parliament
66	P.O.	Post Office
67	N.W.	north-west
68	H.Q.	headquarters

Choose from each bracket the word which will make the statement correct.

69 Wrist is to hand as (toe, ankle, leg) is to foot.

70 House is to man as (barn, shed, sty) is to pig.

71 Sun is to day as (moon, stars, dark) is to night.

72 Foot is to man as (hoof, tusk, paw) is to dog.

73 Bat is to cricket as (paddle, racquet, yacht) is to tennis.

74 Pen is to ink as (brush, pot, box) is to paint.

What do the following expressions mean?

75	black and blue	badly bruised	to be polite
76	a white elephant	something useless	badly bruised
77	to be in hot water	to be in trouble	smart and clean
78	to mind one's Ps and Qs	to be polite	to make a new start
79	a red letter day	an important day	something useless
80	spick and span	smart and clean	an important day
81	to turn over a new leaf	to make a new start	to be in trouble

After each of the following lines write a word that means the same as the word in heavy type.

82 The sailors were told to **abandon** ship. ......leave......

83 The airman received an award for his **heroic** deed. ......brave......

84 I have **sufficient** money to buy it. ......enough......

85 She **inquired** how long she would have to wait. ......asked......

86 The **entire** school went on the outing. ......whole......

87 The children **dispersed** in all directions. ......scattered......

88 The soldier **encountered** many difficulties. ......met/faced......

89–100 See if you can fill in the missing words in this poem.

The chief defect of Kenneth Plumb
Was chewing too much bubble-......gum.......
He chewed away with all his ......might......
Morning, evening, noon and ......night.......
Even, oh! it makes you ......creep (or weep)......
Blowing bubbles in his sleep.
He simply could not get enough,
His face was covered with the ......stuff.......
As for his teeth – oh! what a ......sight......,
It was a wonder he could bite,
His loving mother and his dad
Both remonstrated with the ......lad.......
Ken repaid them for the trouble
By blowing yet another ......bubble......

Kenneth by Wendy Cope

A defect is a: hobby, <u>fault</u>, game, reflection
Remonstrated means: <u>protested</u>, stated, talked, laughed
His teeth became: white, unwashed, <u>decayed</u>, false
This was because he: was hungry, <u>ate too much sugar</u>, was lonely, could not sleep

Underline the right answers.

Four o'clock strikes,
There's a rising hum,
Then the doors fly open,
The children come.
With a wild cat call
And a hop-scotch hop
And a bouncing ball
And a whirling top.
Grazing of knees,
A hair-pull and a slap,
A hitched-up satchel
A pulled down cap.

Bully boys reeling off,
Hurt ones squealing off,
Aviators wheeling off,
Mousy ones stealing off.
Woollen gloves for chilblains,
Cotton rags for snufflers,
Pig-tails, coat-tails,
Tails of mufflers.
Thinning away now
By some and some.
Thinning away, away.
All gone home.

Four o'clock by Hal Summers

1   The children are coming out of (a shop, a cinema, <u>a school</u>)

2   What time is it? (<u>Four o'clock</u>, nine o'clock, I don't know)

3   What time of the year is it? (Summer, <u>winter</u>, I don't know)

4   "A rising hum" is (the noise coming from a high building, someone humming in a high voice, <u>a noise getting louder</u>)

5   "Cotton rags" are for (<u>people with colds</u>, people who take snuff, people with chilblains)

6   "Tails of mufflers" are (tails of pet mice, <u>ends of scarves</u>, tails of pigs)

7   The quiet children are called (<u>the mousy ones</u>, the hurt ones, snufflers, aviators)

8   The cyclists are called (bully boys, <u>aviators</u>, those with pulled down caps)

9   Another word for crying is (whirling, wheeling, <u>squealing</u>, reeling)

10   In the poem, to go off quietly is called (<u>stealing</u>, reeling, thinning, wheeling)

The answers to these clues can be made from letters in the word **sycamore.**

11   alike   same

12   arrived   came

13   container case

14   a planet   Mars

Write one word for each definition:

15   Part of a plant that grows downwards and draws food from the soil.   root

16   The time between noon and evening   afternoon

17   A grown-up person   adult

18   A member of the army   soldier

19   A small, white flower which often grows in meadows   daisy

20   A line of people, one behind another, waiting for their turn to do something.   queue

12

Instead of the word in heavy type, write a word which rhymes with it to make a sensible sentence.

21   In the band he played the **numb** ....drum....

22   He asked **cow** ....how.... he should do it.

23   They climbed on to a **how** ....bough.... of the oak tree.

24   She had a nasty **team** ....dream.... last night.

25   Dad put a **table** ....label.... on the luggage.

In each of the following lines, underline the word which has an opposite meaning to the word on the left.

26   **good**   unhappy   <u>bad</u>   unpleasant   silly

27   **clean**   <u>dirty</u>   washed   unhealthy   ill

28   **hot**   chilly   windy   <u>cold</u>   warm

29   **winter**   spring   hot   weather   <u>summer</u>

30   **day**   <u>night</u>   evening   noon   dawn

31   **shallow**   fat   lean   <u>deep</u>   swallow

32   **difficult** impossible   hard   problem   <u>easy</u>

Write each of the following in the past tense.

33   The man catches a fish.   The man caught a fish.

34   Tom begins his homework.   Tom began his homework.

35   Sandra is not well.   Sandra was not well.

36   The children see the circus.   The children saw the circus.

What noises do animals make?

37   A dog ....barks....   38   A bull ....bellows....

39   A donkey ....brays....   40   A cat ....purrs/mews....

41   A lamb ....bleats....   42   A bear ....growls....

43   A monkey ....chatters....   44   A lion ....roars....

45   A frog ....croaks....

13

Make adjectives from the following words:

46 friend   a _friendly_ girl

47 wood   a _wooden_ box

48 winter   a _wintry_ scene

49 nature   a _natural_ look

50 tide   a _tidal_ wave

51 sense   a _sensible_ answer

52 help   a _helpful_ nurse

53 music   a _musical_ instrument

In each of the following lines underline the word that does not fit in with the rest.

54 football   cricket   netball   <u>pitch</u>   tennis

55 tights   <u>hair</u>   coat   shoes   hat

56 nose   teeth   nails   toes   <u>wool</u>

57 desk   blackboard   <u>bed</u>   chalk   book

58 plate   cup   saucer   <u>kettle</u>   dish

59 primrose   <u>ash</u>   violet   snowdrop   crocus

Write the words in heavy type in the past tense.

60–61 We **see** _saw_ the paper which the man **holds** _held_

62–63 Tom **buys** _bought_ a pen which he **gives** _gave_ to his cousin.

64–65 I **write** _wrote_ a letter which my brother **posts** _posted_

66–67 Andrew **wins** _won_ the prize which the vicar **presents** _presented_

68–69 I **walk** _walked_ to school quickly but Jane **catches** _caught_ me up.

Underline the adjectives.

70–75 The <u>spoiled</u> boy had a <u>red, tearful</u> face as his <u>tired</u> mother said she could not afford the <u>new electric</u> car.

14

Give the plural of the following words.

76 box boxes **77** potato potatoes **78** tooth teeth

79 mouse mice **80** lady ladies **81** sheep sheep

82 foot feet **83** knife knives **84** woman women

What would you expect to find

85 in a kettle? water

86 in a vase? flowers

87 in an envelope? letter

88 in a purse? money

89 in a satchel? books

90 in a garage? car

Underline the correct word in brackets.

91–92 The (scent, <u>sent</u>) of the flowers you (scent, <u>sent</u>) me is strong.

93–94 Tom (<u>threw</u>, through) the ball (<u>through</u>, threw) the window.

95–96 The (not, <u>knot</u>) joining these ropes is (<u>not</u>, knot) tied tightly.

97–98 Michelle cut her hand on the (pain, <u>pane</u>) of glass and the (pane, <u>pain</u>) is very bad.

99–100 I saw him (stair, <u>stare</u>) at the man on the (stare, <u>stair</u>).

Paper 4

Underline the right answers.

Finger painting

Collect several small containers, and use one for each colour. Start with white which is the most useful colour and use your largest container for it. Take 6 spoonfuls of paint and mix it with 4 spoonfuls of paste and 4 spoonfuls of water. Mix with a spoon or stick. Remember the paint must be thick. Prepare the other colours in the same way using 3 spoonfuls of paint and 2 spoonfuls each of paste and water.

white + a little dark blue = sky blue   yellow + dark blue = green
white + a little red = pink   red + dark blue = violet
white + a little black = grey

See what other shades you can make.

1   In finger painting which is the most useful colour?
(White, black, they are all the same)

2   Stir the mixture with (a knife, your finger, a stick)

3–4   Which two colours make green? (Blue, red, yellow, white)

5 If you wanted a paler green you would add
(water, <u>white paint</u>, blue paint, yellow paint)

6–7 Which two colours make grey? (<u>Black</u>, red, <u>white</u>, blue)

8 If you wanted a darker grey you would add
(<u>black paint</u>, white paint, water)

9 Red and dark blue make (pink, <u>violet</u>, sky blue)

10 Why do they tell you to make more white mixture than other colours?
(Most things are painted white, it is the cheapest paint, it is the
thickest paint, <u>it is used with other colours to make them lighter</u>)

11 What are you told to use for this painting?
(A brush, <u>your fingers</u>, a spoon)

12–19 The words below can be given an opposite meaning by putting either
im or **un** in front of them. Put them in the right columns.

perfect   happy   dressed   pure   kind   possible   patient   sure

im	**un**
perfect	happy
pure	dressed
possible	kind
patient	sure

Write the correct letters in the spaces.

20–21 Elaine was Mrs. Brown's y ..oung.. est da ..ugh.. ter.

22–23 The fr ..ien.. dly girl helped the old w ..oma.. n across the road.

In each space write the plural of the word on the left.

24 loaf   The lady bought two large ..loaves..

25 sheep   The farmer owned a hundred ..sheep..

26 baby   The ..babies.. were asleep in their prams.

27 goose   The ..geese.. waddled across the yard.

28 thief   The ..thieves.. were caught when they opened the safe.

17

Write the opposite of each word.

29 asleep _awake_   30 raise _lower_   31 careless _careful_

32 hot _cold_   33 autumn _spring_   34 cruel _kind_

Underline the word which is the same part of speech as the word on the left.

35 **us**   children   came   <u>we</u>   go

36 **kick**   football   goal   <u>play</u>   boys

37 **happy**   dog   friend   him   <u>sad</u>

38 **slowly** speed   I   come   <u>quickly</u>

39 **man**   he   <u>aunt</u>   strong   go

40 **their**   there   though   <u>our</u>   through

41 **teach**   <u>learn</u>   children   school   books

From the letters in the word DICTIONARY form other words with the following definitions.

42 A metal _iron_

43 An attack _raid_

44 A locomotive machine _train_

45 A deed _action_ (or act)

46 A measurement _yard_

47 A record of our day _diary_

48 Where milk is bottled _dairy_

49 To shed tears _cry_

Put these towns in alphabetical order.

Norwich   Northwich   Northampton   Nottingham   Norwood   Northallerton

50 (1) _Northallerton_   51 (2) _Northampton_

52 (3) _Northwich_   53 (4) _Norwich_

54 (5) _Norwood_   55 (6) _Nottingham_

18

Underline one word in each of the following lines which includes all the others.

56 doll   teddy-bear   <u>toy</u>   ball   bat

57 London   <u>capital</u>   Edinburgh   Paris   Madrid

58 car   <u>vehicle</u>   coach   bus   lorry

59 <u>time</u>   second   hour   minute   day

60 chair   table   sideboard   desk   <u>furniture</u>

61 tennis   football   cricket   <u>game</u>   hockey

62 piano   <u>instrument</u>   drums   guitar   organ

After each of the following lines write a word that means the same as the word in heavy type.

63 I **attempted** to climb the rock.   tried

64 She was **requested** to sit down and wait.   asked

65 He **remarked** that he was cold and tired.   said

66 The picture **adhered** to the paper.   stuck

67 She **frequently** went to see her grandmother.   often

68 John was **awarded** the first prize.   given

69 Shaun's family was very **wealthy**.   rich

70 At the concert the children **applauded** loudly.   clapped

Underline the pronouns in the following:

71–74 <u>We</u> are going to Hull to see the docks: <u>it</u> should be very interesting.
<u>We</u> will see several ships, and hope to go round <u>them</u>.

Underline the correct spelling.

75 The (lessen, <u>lesson</u>) started at eleven o'clock.

76 The man gave a (<u>groan</u>, grown) as he lifted his arm.

77 Dad said we must get a new ironing (<u>board</u>, bored).

78 The (loan, <u>lone</u>) sailor had crossed the ocean.

79 The gardener put in (steaks, <u>stakes</u>) for the sweet peas to climb up.

Underline the word in each line which rhymes with the word on the left.

80 **though**   cough   rough   <u>so</u>   thought   bought

81 **alone**   <u>thrown</u>   gone   done   along   only

82 **whole**   while   whale   holly   ghost   <u>goal</u>

83 **move**   love   <u>prove</u>   dove   glove   drove

84 **hour**   pour   hair   floor   <u>power</u>   mower

85 **quay**   play   sway   <u>sea</u>   day   fray

86 **few**   mow   <u>grew</u>   sew   saw   claw

87–95 Fill in the missing words in this poem.

September starts a fresh school <u>year</u> ,
New pupils feel a twinge of fear.
Our Harvest Festival's displayed,
Our thanks to farmers duly <u>made</u> .
October's damp; the leaves fall <u>down</u>
We make a book called "Our Home Town".
Big pictures pinned on wall and door;
There's thick mud on the cloakroom <u>floor</u> .
November brings us Bonfire <u>Night</u>
With blazing guy and fireworks <u>bright</u> .
The Christmas plays – rehearsals <u>start</u> ,
Who'll sing songs? Who'll speak a part?
December's cold; there's frost and <u>snow</u>
To "Peter Pan" in town we go.
We decorate the school, have treats;
At parties there are prizes, <u>sweets</u> .

The School Year by Wes Magee

96–100 Look at the words below. Underline any that are spelt wrongly, and write them correctly in the spaces.

receive	<u>beleive</u>	deceive	<u>fourty</u>	ninety
<u>libary</u>	conceit	<u>theif</u>	seize	<u>sheild</u>
believe	forty	library	thief	shield

Underline the right answers.

What is a hobbit? I suppose hobbits need some description nowadays since they have become rare and shy to the Big People, as they call us. They are (or were) a little people, about half our height, and smaller than the bearded Dwarfs. Hobbits have no beards. There is little or no magic about them, except the ordinary everyday sort which helps them to disappear quietly and quickly when large stupid folk like you and me come blundering along, making a noise like elephants which they can hear a mile off. They are inclined to be fat in the stomach; they dress in bright colours (chiefly green and yellow); wear no shoes because their feet grow natural leather soles, and thick warm brown hair like the stuff on their heads (which is curly); have long brown fingers, good natured faces and laugh deep laughs (especially after dinner which they have twice a day when they can get it).

From *The hobbit* by J. R. R. Tolkien

1 What magic can hobbits do? (Make themselves smaller, disappear quickly and quietly, make magic shoes)

2 Hobbits think (elephants, dwarfs, people) make a lot of noise.

3-4 They don't need shoes because (their feet have leathery soles, they don't go out, the hair on their feet keeps them warm, they are too fat)

5-8 Hobbits have (brown hair, bald heads, curly hair, beards, long fingers, pleasant faces)

9 The skin of a hobbit is (white, pink, black, brown, I don't know)

10 Do hobbits enjoy their food? (Yes, no, I don't know)

21

Form nouns from the words on the left.

11   deep   Before you dive into water you should know its ...depth...

12   wide   The ...width... of the bath is twenty metres.

13   sell   We bought a washing machine in the ...sale...

14-18   Alter this sentence, putting into direct speech what she actually said. Don't forget the punctuation and capital letters!

She asked him if he had cut the grass.

She said, "Have you cut the grass?"

If you re-arrange the letters at the end of each line they will give you the correct word to write in each space.

19   It was a lovely, warm, ...sunny... day and I   ynsun

20   was sitting in the ...garden... reading a   aenrdg

21   book. After a time I fell ...asleep...   saplee

22   I had an exciting ...dream... in which   madre

23   I found some ...hidden... treasure. I   eiddnh

24   was very ...sorry... when Mum called me   rrsyo

25   to say it was ...time... for tea.   mtei

26   Lamb is to sheep as foal is to ...horse...

27   Stand is to sit as up is to ...down...

28   Finger is to hand as toe is to ...foot...

29   Aunt is to niece as uncle is to ...nephew...

30   Open is to shut as clever is to ...stupid...

31   Glove is to hand as ...shoe... is to foot.

Underline the word which is opposite in meaning to the word on the left.

32 **open**   unlatched   <u>closed</u>   ready   wide

33 **false**   fancy   funny   <u>true</u>   teeth

34 **future**   <u>past</u>   present   time   age

35 **seldom**   selfish   always   <u>often</u>   never

36 **expensive** good   <u>cheap</u>   price   cost

37 **tender**   smart   sender   <u>tough</u>   gentle

38 **forgot**   thought   think   forget   <u>remembered</u>

Fill in the spaces with nouns linked to the words on the left.

39 proud   He took great ....pride........ in his new bicycle.

40 invent   His ......invention...... became world famous.

41 deep   The man measured the ......depth...... of the water.

42 live   The ......life...... of the President was in danger.

43 attend   Her ......attendance...... at school was very good.

Complete the following table of adjectives of comparison.

Example: good   better   best

		better	best
44–45	quick	quicker	quickest
46–47	plain	plainer	plainest
48–49	few	fewer	fewest
50–51	old	older	oldest
52–53	dry	drier	driest
54–55	small	smaller	smallest

Write either **as** or **has** in each space—whichever you think makes sense.

56–57 Tom cannot sing ......as...... he ......has...... a sore throat.

58–59 The girl said that her hands were ......as...... cold ......as...... ice.

60–61 " ......Has...... he done ......as...... he was told?"

62–63 " ......Has...... she told you that she ......has...... a headache?"

64–65 Joanne ran ......as...... fast ......as...... she could.

Complete the following proverbs by choosing a word from the column at the right of the page.

66	A stitch in time saves _nine_	fire
67	It is no use crying over spilt _milk_	work
68	Where there's a will there's a _way_	speed
69	Two heads are better than _one_	milk
70	Many hands make light _work_	nine
71	More haste less _speed_	way
72	Out of the frying pan into the _fire_	one

Underline a word in each line which is similar in meaning to the word on the left.

73	**permit**	stop	leave	<u>allow</u>	admit
74	**interior**	outside	<u>inside</u>	back	front
75	**imitate**	<u>copy</u>	like	imagine	draw
76	**expense**	expect	<u>cost</u>	money	charge
77	**pardon**	forget	permit	let	<u>forgive</u>

Give ONE word for each of these definitions:

78	Can be used when eating. It has two, three or four prongs set on the end of a handle.	It is a _fork_
79	A period of two weeks	It is a _fortnight_
80	A network of fine threads spun by a spider to catch insects	It is a _web_
81	A big, four-legged animal with tusks, and a long trunk	It is an _elephant_
82	A doll worked by pulling wires or strings in a toy theatre	It is a _puppet_
83	Made by birds as a place in which to lay eggs and bring up their young	It is a _nest_
84	A raised platform on which plays are often produced	It is a _stage_
85	Thin rope, line or cord used for tying up parcels	It is _string_

Write either **there** or **their** in each of the blanks.

86 I would like to go ....there.... today.

87 ....There.... was someone in the waiting room.

88 I like the colour of ....their.... school uniform.

89 "What a lot of work ....there.... is to do," said Mum.

90–91 The children were told to put ....their.... books inside ....their.... desks.

92 "Stand ....there....," said the policeman.

93–94 They put ....their.... books over ....there....

Underline a word in each line which best describes the word on the left.

95 **river**   red   <u>wide</u>   good   useful

96 **sky**   old   nice   <u>stormy</u>   ugly

97 **clock**   <u>alarm</u>   date   warm   bed

98 **kitten**   great   short   long   <u>tiny</u>

99 **boat**   real   <u>motor</u>   simple   bright

100 **fire**   pink   cold   <u>coal</u>   busy

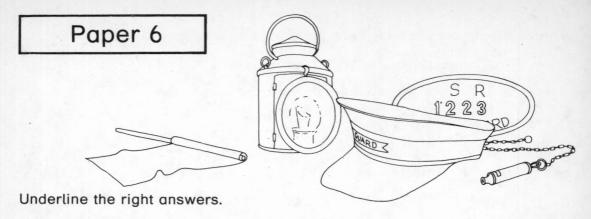

Underline the right answers.

I remember the long homeward ride, begun
By the light that slanted in from the level sun;
And on the far embankment, in sunny heat,
Our whole train's shadow travelling dark and complete.
A farmer snored. Two loud gentlemen spoke
Of the cricket and news. The pink baby awoke
And gurgled awhile. Till slowly out of the day
The last light sank in glimmer and ashy-grey.
I remember it all; and dimly remember, too,
The place where we changed—the dark trains lumbering through;
The refreshment room, the crumbs, and the slopped tea;
And the salt on my face, not of tears, not tears, but the sea.
"Our train at last!" said Father. "Now tumble in!
It's the last lap home!" And I wondered what "lap" could mean;
But the rest is all lost, for a huge drowsiness crept
Like a yawn upon me; I leant against Mother and slept.

Journey home by John Walsh

1   How was I travelling? (In a car, in a train, in a bus)

2–3   The weather was (hot, cold, grey, sunny, stormy)

4–5   In the poem two people slept. They were (the baby, the gentlemen, a farmer, me)

6   Was the baby happy? (Yes, no, I do not know)

7   "The place where we changed." What did we change? (Seats, clothes, trains, homes)

8   When we waited for the second train we went to (the refreshment room, the sea, the embankment)

9   Where was I going? (To the seaside, to my home, to a farm)

10   Where do you think I had been? (To school, to see my parents, for a holiday)

11   What time of day was it? (Evening, morning, noon, midnight)

12   "The last lap" means (the person I leant against, a race, the last part of the journey home)

Choose an adverb from the column on the right.

13   In the race the boy ran ....swiftly....   suddenly

14   Kim wrote the letter very ....neatly....   neatly

15   The old tramp ate his food ....greedily....   heavily

16   All day the rain fell ....heavily....   soundly

17   The child slept ....soundly....   smartly

18   The car braked ....suddenly....   greedily

19   The young lady dressed ....smartly....   swiftly

The noises made by animals are given different names. For example, a dog barks. Write the name given to the noises made by the following animals.

20   a duck ....quacks....   21   turkeys ....gobble....

22   a sheep ....bleats....   23   geese ....cackle....

24   an elephant ....trumpets....   25   a sparrow ....chirps....

In each line, underline the correct word in the brackets.

26   On (Teusday, Tuesday, Tusday) I go to the Youth Club.

27   "Pass me a (peace, peice, piece) of bread, please."

28   Of (coarse, course, corse) he can come to tea.

29   Jane (rote, wrought, wrote) an exciting poem.

30   The dog (lay, laid, layed) on the hearth-rug.

31   Pete (through, throw, threw) a cricket ball.

Arrange the following words in dictionary order.

pain   pail   pale   paint   pair   paper

32   (1) ....pail....   33   (2) ....pain....   34   (3) ....paint....

35   (4) ....pair....   36   (5) ....pale....   37   (6) ....paper....

What do the following expressions mean? Underline the correct answer.

38   hard up (very hard, short of money, at the top)

39   to get into hot water (to get into trouble, to bath, to wash in hot water)

40   to have forty winks (to blink, to play winking, to have a short sleep)

41   to go on all fours (to go to each corner, to ride a horse, to crawl on hands and knees)

42   to play with fire (to ask for trouble, to light fireworks, to put coal on the fire)

43   to play the game (to do P.E., to act fairly, to play when you should work)

44   to lead a dog's life (to live in a kennel, to crawl about, to be treated badly)

Write one word which will describe all the things on each line.
Example: arm   leg   hand   foot   **limbs**

45   socks   vests   blouses   shirts   clothes

46   offices   houses   shops   churches   buildings

47   franc   cent   penny   dollar   money/coins

48   beetle   ant   wasp   bee   insects

49   hammer   chisel   spanner   saw   tools

50   ring   watch   necklace   bracelet   jewellery

In each pair of spaces write two words which sound the same but are spelled differently.
Example: She had to **wait** at the station.
       The **weight** was great.

51–52   She broke a ....pane.... of glass.

        She had a ....pain.... in her side.

53–54   I brush and comb my ....hair....

        A ....hare.... is a small animal.

55–56   He ....knew.... where to look for his bat.

        "Look at my ....new.... dress," said Meena.

57–58 I have a ...pear... and an apple.

George has lost a ...pair... of shoes.

Underline the correct word among those in brackets.

59 A kitchen never has   (a sink, a stove, a table, a car)

60 A rose never has   (leaves, knives, buds, a stem)

61 A chair never has   (legs, a back, a clock, a seat)

62 A book never has   (a light, pages, paper, a cover)

63 A bus never has   (a door, seats, legs, a driver)

64–75 In the following passage every sixth word has been left out. Can you fill them in?

Rain and wind, and wind ...and... rain.

Will the summer come ...again... ?

Rain on houses, on the ...street... ,

Wetting all the people's feet.

...Though... they run with might and ...main... ,

Rain and wind, and wind ...and... rain.

Snow and sleet, and ...sleet... and snow.

Will the winter ...never... go?

What do beggar children ...do...

With no fire to cuddle ...to... ,

P'raps with nowhere warm to ...go... ?

Snow and sleet, and sleet ...and... snow.

Join the two parts of each of the following sentences with one of these words.
so   but   and   because

76 David likes his tea very hot ...but... Miranda doesn't like tea at all.

77 I couldn't sing ...because... I had a sore throat.

78 Kerry has cut her finger ...so... she will have to bandage it.

79 I am very keen on swimming ...and... I like diving too.

80 The opposite of **depart** is ....arrive........

81 The opposite of **lengthen** is ....shorten........

82 The opposite of **buy** is ....sell........

83 The opposite of **find** is ....lose........

84 The opposite of **grow** is ....shrink........

85 The opposite of **soften** is ....harden........

Underline the word which rhymes with the word on the left.

86 **buy**   day   bay   <u>tie</u>   toy

87 **lane**   lean   thin   clean   <u>rain</u>

88 **want**   need   don't   <u>font</u>   faint

89 **know**   now   <u>so</u>   how   known

90 **said**   talk   laid   paid   <u>bed</u>

91 **knife** <u>life</u>   fork   knit   know

92 **voice** vice   mice   mouse   <u>choice</u>

Underline the correct word in the brackets.

93 None of the girls (were, <u>was</u>) there.

94 Every boy (were, <u>was</u>) on the field.

95 (Their, There, <u>They're</u>) late today.

96 (Were, <u>Where</u>, We're) did you find the book?

97 All the men (<u>were</u>, was) working.

98 You and (me, <u>I</u>) must hurry.

99 I dropped the bag but not one of the eggs (have, <u>has</u>) broken.

100 The boys have (drank, <u>drunk</u>) all the milk.

Underline the right answers.

Not long ago, there lived in London a young married couple of Dalmatian dogs named Pongo and Missis Pongo. (Missis had added Pongo's name to her own on their marriage, but was still called Missis by most people.) They were lucky enough to own a young married couple of humans named Mr. and Mrs. Dearly, who were gentle, obedient, and usually intelligent—almost canine at times. They understood quite a number of barks: the barks for "Out, please!", "In, please!", "Hurry up with my dinner!" and "What about a walk?" And even when they could not understand, they could often guess—if looked at soulfully or scratched by an eager paw. Like many other much-loved humans, they believed that they owned their dogs, instead of realising that their dogs owned them. Pongo and Missis found this touching and amusing and let their pets think it was true.

From *101 Dalmatians* by Dodie Smith

1–2 The dogs' names were (Dalmatian, Pongo, Dearly, Missis)

3–4 Their owners' names were (Mr. Dearly, Mrs. Dearly, Missis, Pongo)

5–7 Their owners (were kind, were old, were slow, did what they were told, were unintelligent, were usually understanding)

8 If the Dearlys didn't understand they (did what they were told, played with the dogs, guessed what they wanted)

9 The dogs had several barks. How many were commands? (1, 2, 3, 4, 5)

10 How many were questions? (1, 2, 3, 4, 5)

11 Pongo and Missis were "touched and amused". Why?
(The Dearlys believed they owned the dogs, they believed that Pongo and Missis owned them, the pets were faithful)

31

12 "Touched" means (they scratched with their paws, <u>they got a pleasant feeling</u>, they pecked at things)

13 "Canine" means (like a can, like a cat, <u>like a dog</u>)

Underline the correct word in the brackets.

14 They picked some bluebells in a country (lain, <u>lane</u>).

15 Dad told Kevin not to (<u>meddle</u>, medal) with the tools.

16 The class was told to (<u>find</u>, fined) the answer.

17 The cat's (fir, <u>fur</u>) was black and shiny.

18 She found a pretty red (bury, <u>berry</u>) on the tree.

Put a ring round the word which has the same meaning as the word on the left, and underline the word which has the opposite meaning.

19–20	**cease**	(stop)	crease	<u>continue</u>	go	call
21–22	**alive**	lonely	(living)	dreary	<u>dead</u>	healthy
23–24	**grief**	(sorrow)	great	graze	song	<u>joy</u>
25–26	**discovered**	shield	<u>lost</u>	(found)	cover	place
27–28	**lift**	<u>lower</u>	high	low	stairs	(raise)

Here are some statements. Some are about elephants and some are about lions. Write **E** after the ones about elephants and **L** after those about lions.

29 They are trained to work in the forests. ....E.......

30 They live in groups called prides. ....L.......

31 The males have manes. ....L.......

32 They have tusks. ....E.......

33 They have golden-brown coats. ....L.......

34 They can push trees down with their trunks. ....E.......

35 They are called the King of Animals. ....L.......

36 They make a trumpetting noise. ....E.......

37 They have a thick grey skin. ....E.......

38 They belong to the cat family. ....L.......

Underline the word which is opposite in meaning to the word on the left.

39 **export**   goods   <u>import</u>   duty   business

40 **sell**   charge   shop   customer   <u>buy</u>

41 **heavy**   <u>light</u>   weight   load   heave

42 **exit**   go   out   excite   <u>entrance</u>

43 **future**   passed   tomorrow   <u>past</u>   evening

Complete the words below by adding either **able** or **ible** to the end.

44 pay _able_   45 irrit _able_   46 divis _ible_

47 cap _able_   48 invis _ible_   49 work _able_

The answers to the following are all 4-lettered words beginning
with the letter **t.**

50 It grows in gardens   t _ree_   51 Not wild   t _ame_
   and parks

52 To get exhausted   t _ire_   53 A story   t _ale_

54 Ripped   t _ore_   55 Not false   t _rue_

56 Toothpaste is often in one   t _ube_

Re-write the following, changing all the underlined words from the singular
to the plural.

57–59 The <u>dwarf</u> ran to <u>his</u> tiny <u>house</u>.

............_The dwarfs ran to their tiny houses._............

60–62 The <u>roof</u> of the <u>factory</u> <u>was</u> red.

............_The roofs of the factories were red._............

63–64 The <u>wolf</u> drew near the <u>city</u>.

............_The wolves drew near the cities._............

Underline the word in the brackets which means the same as the word in
heavy type.

65 The girl was very **fortunate** to have such a beautiful bicycle.
   (Fated, <u>lucky</u>, unlucky, afraid)

66 It was a very **dismal** day. (Dirty, wet, <u>dull</u>, dry)

67 The results of the tests **astonished** everyone.
(<u>Surprised</u>, praised, expected, pleased)

68 The boy was **insolent** to his teacher. (Polite, helpful, kind, <u>rude</u>)

69 The work **commenced** last week. (Finished, <u>started</u>, continued)

In each line, underline a word which is the same part of speech as the word on the left.

70	**toy**	black	little	small	playful	<u>wolf</u>
71	**see**	six	sight	<u>give</u>	day	us
72	**our**	boy	girl	hour	<u>my</u>	hot
73	**happily**	sweet	<u>quickly</u>	sing	laugh	games
74	**good**	girl	<u>hungry</u>	as	book	she

In each line underline a word which means the same as the word on the left.

75	**rapid**	race	slow	<u>quick</u>	crawl
76	**join**	part	<u>unite</u>	joint	crack
77	**govern**	<u>rule</u>	country	nation	cover
78	**quantity**	less	little	<u>amount</u>	more
79	**dusk**	morning	night	sun	<u>twilight</u>
80	**remedy**	pain	<u>cure</u>	remain	illness

Form nouns from the words on the left.

81 sad   There was much ....<u>sadness</u>........ and suffering.

82 act   His quick ....<u>action</u>........ saved her life.

83 absent   Her ....<u>absence</u>........ made things very difficult.

84 angry   The boy's ....<u>anger</u>........ was aroused when he saw the
dog being ill-treated.

85 fly   The birds prepared for their ....<u>flight</u>........

Underline the correct word in the brackets.

86 Your pencil-box is bigger (<u>than</u>, from, to) mine.

87 Sarah agreed (that, <u>with</u>, to, from) Lisa.

88 Paul's peg is stronger (from, <u>than</u>, to) mine.

89 George's knife is similar (from, <u>to</u>, than) mine.

90 John's coat is different (<u>from</u>, to, than) Pat's.

Put each word on the left into the past tense.

91 shine   Yesterday the sun ....shone.... brightly.

92 fight   In 1815, Napoleon ....fought.... against the English.

93 sing   We all ....sang.... carols last Christmas Eve.

94 dig   The man ....dug.... up the lawn and planted some vegetables.

95 eat   We had a lovely picnic and ....ate.... lots of sandwiches.

Punctuate the following by putting an apostrophe in each line.

96 "Tom's got a new anorak."

97 "Where's your basket?"

98 "Isn't it there?"

99 "You'll do it soon."

100 "Don't do that!"

Paper 8

Underline the right answers.

I dared not stir out of my castle for days, lest some savage should capture me. However, I gained a little courage and went with much dread to make sure that the footprint was not my own. I measured my foot against it. Mine was not nearly so large. A stranger, maybe a savage, must have been on shore, and fear again filled my heart.

I determined now to make my house more secure than ever. I built another wall round it, in which I fixed six guns, so that, if need be, I could fire off six in two minutes. Then I planted young trees around. I feared my goats might be hurt or stolen from me, so I fenced round several plots of ground, as much out of sight as possible, and put some goats in each plot. All this while I lived with a terrible fear in my mind that I might one day meet an enemy. I had lived on this lonely island for eighteen years.

Once, when on the opposite side of the island, I was filled with horror; for on the ground I saw the remains of a fire, and also a number of human bones. This told me plainly that cannibals had been there.

From *Robinson Crusoe* by Daniel Defoe

1 How did I know the footprint was not mine? (It was smaller than mine, it was larger than mine, it was a strange shape)

2 What did I plant round my house? (A wall, guns, young trees)

3 What did I build round my house? (A fire, a fence, another wall)

4 How did I protect my goats? (By firing guns, by planting trees, by fencing round their plots)

5 What was my greatest fear? (That I might meet an enemy, that I would be burned, that I would be shot)

6 What did I fix to the wall? (Young trees, a chimney, six guns)

7–8 What did I see on the opposite side of the island? (Enemies, cannibals, human bones, savages, the remains of a fire)

9 What told me that cannibals had been on the island? (The sight of human bones, a footprint, a fire)

10 How long had I been on the island? (A few days, eighteen years, I don't know)

Choose the most suitable word from the column on the right to write in each space.

11 The ....howling.... of the wind   rustling

12 The ....rumbling.... of thunder   clanking

13 The ....shuffling.... of feet   lapping

14 The ....lapping.... of the waves   howling

15 The ....clanking.... of chains   shuffling

16 The ....rustling.... of leaves   rumbling

17–22 Underline the adjectives (describing words) which are in the following sentence:

The beautiful, young queen took her golden scissors and cut a piece of coloured material, and made a pretty, little bag for the princess.

23–27 Underline the adverbs in the following.

The old lady walked slowly up the hill. She met a small boy who was singing happily as he cycled quickly to school. In the sweetshop the man spoke crossly to the girl who was leaning lazily against the counter.

Underline the correct answers.

28 **Ship-shape** means
(shaped like a boat, seaworthy, <u>neat and tidy</u>)

29 **To make believe** means
(<u>to pretend</u>, to understand, to pray, to tell)

30 **A wet blanket** means
(damp bedclothes, <u>a miserable person</u>, low clouds)

31 **Under the weather** means
(walking in the rain, carrying an umbrella, <u>not feeling well</u>)

32 **Fit as a fiddle** means
(playing a violin, <u>healthy</u>, musical)

33 **Look before you leap** means
(to jump over puddles, <u>to think before you act</u>, to be good at long jumping)

Underline the word which is opposite in meaning to the word on the left.

34 **polite**   pleasant   thankful   <u>rude</u>   police

35 **guilty**   <u>innocent</u>   bad   dirty   happy

36 **stationary**   paper   <u>moving</u>   still   quiet

37 **plenty**   much   more   some   <u>scarce</u>

38 **strong**   heavy   <u>weak</u>   little   fat

39 **expand**   <u>contract</u>   enlarge   small   size

40 **future**   present   happening   <u>past</u>   event

Write the past tense of each word on the left.

41 speak   We ...<u>spoke</u>... to her about it.

42 hide   John ...<u>hid</u>... the thimble under the cushion.

43 write   Sharon ...<u>wrote</u>... all her party invitations.

44 catch   Daniel ...<u>caught</u>... measles, and David did too.

45 shake   They ...<u>shook</u>... with fright.

46 sing   Thomas ...<u>sang</u>... a solo at the concert.

38

Squirrels are found in most countries. In Europe it is the red squirrel that is seen most, but in Britain the grey squirrel has been introduced from America. Flying squirrels do not really fly but glide from one tree to another. Ground squirrels may dig large numbers of burrows, and these make "a town".

47-51   Underline the statements below which are true.

There are only grey squirrels in Britain.
Flying squirrels glide.
Grey squirrels first came from America.
Squirrels are only found in Europe.
There are not many squirrels now.
A squirrel's home is called a burrow.
Flying squirrels live in America only.
Many burrows make a town.
The most common squirrel in Europe is the red squirrel.

Some colours have been left out of the following verse. Each colour is mentioned twice. Can you fill them in?

52-63   What is pink? A rose is pink
By the fountain's brink.

What is ......red..... ? A poppy's ......red......
In its barley bed.

What is ...blue... ? The sky is ...blue...
Where the clouds float through.

What is ...white... ? A swan is ...white...
Sailing in the light.

What is ...yellow... ? Pears are ...yellow...
Rich and ripe and mellow.

What is ...green... ? The grass is ...green...
With small flowers in between.

What is ...orange... ? Why, an ...orange...
Just an orange.

Underline the correct word in brackets.

64 Each of the children (have, <u>has</u>) a pencil.

65 None of the girls (were, <u>was</u>) present.

66 All the boys (<u>were</u>, was) early.

67 Neither of the goalkeepers (were, <u>was</u>) hurt.

68 Most of the boys (<u>have</u>, has) a bicycle.

In each space, write an adjective related to the word on the left.

69 patience   *patient*   70 silence   *silent*

71 strength   *strong*   72 friend   *friendly*

73 kindness   *kind*   74 heat   *hot*

75 crowd   *crowded*

Use a word from the column on the right to fill each space.

76 A breath of *air*   water

77 A blade of *grass*   grass

78 A pinch of *salt*   salt

79 A pat of *butter*   butter

80 A drop of *water*   sand

81 A grain of *sand*   air

Underline two words in each line which have something in common with the word on the left.

82–83	**bed**	<u>mattress</u>	dress	<u>sheet</u>	window
84–85	**book**	<u>page</u>	parcel	price	<u>chapter</u>
86–87	**kitchen**	bed	<u>sink</u>	<u>oven</u>	tidy
88–89	**car**	useful	<u>engine</u>	large	<u>brakes</u>
90–91	**Christmas**	room	<u>carols</u>	<u>cards</u>	spring
92–93	**day**	work	<u>morning</u>	lazy	<u>afternoon</u>
94–95	**bicycle**	clothes	hammer	<u>pedals</u>	<u>wheels</u>

Underline the conjunctions, or joining words.

96 I am going home soon <u>but</u> he is going to stay here.

97 The dog has a collar <u>and</u> a lead.

98 They waited <u>until</u> the train arrived.

99 Marion was going to school <u>when</u> I saw her.

100 David knew John was there <u>because</u> he had seen him.

Underline the right answers.

Many animals are camouflaged by being the same colour as the places where they live. The polar bear who lives in the snowy far north has white fur. The kangaroo, who lives in dry, dusty grassland, has sandy-coloured fur. The colour of the lion blends in with the colour of dried up grass found in hot countries. The tapirs, who live in the jungles, have a colour pattern which seems of little use—the front of their bodies, their heads and their legs are black, while the rest is white. We can pick out tapirs easily at the zoo but in their homeland it is not so. They hunt at night when there are patches of moonlight and patches of shadow and this is how they are protected. Some animals, like the Arctic fox, who live in cold countries change the colour of their coats in winter so that the new white coat will tone in with the snow. Other animals have a dazzle pattern. A zebra's black and white stripes don't blend in with its surroundings, but zebras feed in the early morning and late evening when they cannot be seen so well. Their outline is broken up against the tall grasses and trees and they become almost invisible.

1   Camouflage is (a background, a disguise, a colour)

2–3   A kangaroo (has a coat which blends in with dried up grass, lives in the desert, has a sand-coloured coat, lives in the jungle)

4   The coat of which animal changes colour in winter?
(Bear, zebra, tapir, fox)

5–7   A tapir (lives in the jungle, hunts during the day, is striped, is half black and half white, hunts late)

8   The (fox, zebra, tapir, kangaroo, lion) has a dazzle pattern.

9   Which animal lives in a hot country and has a coat the colour of dried up grass? (<u>Lion</u>, tiger, tapir)

10–11   Which animals are black and white? (Lion, <u>zebra</u>, fox, kangaroo, <u>tapir</u>)

12   Why don't farmyard animals and pets have to have a camouflage? Because (our weather is always changing, <u>they don't have to hide</u>, we are too close to them)

Form nouns linked with the words on the left.

13   think   It was a kind <u>thought</u>

14   visit   The <u>visitor</u> was shown round the school.

15   enter   The <u>entrance</u> is on High Street.

16   sit   The <u>seat</u> was very comfortable.

17   amuse   The clown caused much <u>amusement</u>

Underline one word in each line which does not fit in with the others.

18   snow   frost   hail   <u>sun</u>   ice

19   brave   noble   courageous   good   <u>weak</u>

20   boat   <u>ball</u>   ship   yacht   canoe

21   rope   cord   <u>needle</u>   twine   string

In the first column write a word which means the same as the word on the left. In the second column write a word which means the opposite.

	1st column	2nd column
22–23 difficult	hard	easy
24–25 interior	inside	outside/exterior
26–27 stern	strict	lenient
28–29 reveal	show	conceal/hide
30–31 prohibit	forbid	allow

Can you complete the following five-letter words with the following definitions? They all begin with the letters CR.

32 CR _owd_ a lot of people

33 CR _own_ the Queen sometimes wears one

34 CR _oak_ the noise made by frogs

35 CR _ash_ to fall with a loud noise

36 CR _ook_ a stick with a hooked top used by shepherds

37 CR _ane_ a wading bird; a machine for lifting heavy weights

38 CR _isp_ a thin slice of potato

Look at these pairs of words. If they are alike in meaning write an A. If they are opposite, write an O.

39 author, reader ....O....

40 fault, error ....A....

41 here, there ....O....

42 win, lose ....O....

43 confess, admit ....A....

44 gap, hole ....A....

45 kind, cruel ....O....

46 teacher, pupil ....O....

47 eager, keen ....A....

48 question, answer ....O....

Complete each line with a word linked to the one on the left.

49 tell It was an exciting story he ....told....

50 fell The ....fall.... of snow was very heavy.

51 begin The ....beginning.... of the book was not interesting.

52 enjoy It was worth making the effort to see their ....enjoyment....

Underline the correct word in brackets.

53 They (drank, drunk) their milk.

54 She cannot do (no, any) more.

55 Mr. Scott gave it to Tim and (I, me).

56-57 Neither Vicky (or, nor) Paul (has, have) a book.

58 None of the children (is, are) ready.

Complete each sentence by choosing a group of words from the following.

> rough and ready   head and shoulders
> wear and tear   odds and ends

59   Jane's winter coat was showing signs of ....*wear and tear*........

60   There were lots of ....*odds and ends*........ at the Jumble Sale.

61   Dean was ....*head and shoulders*........ taller than Christopher.

62   The repair looked very ....*rough and ready*........

63–67   Choose the most suitable of these words to fill in each of the blanks in the passage below.

> arrived   accepted   performance   invitation   pleasure

I was very glad to receive an ....*invitation*........ to the school concert, and I ....*accepted*........ it with ....*pleasure*........ When I ....*arrived*........ at the hall it was nearly time for the ....*performance*........ to begin.

68–73   Give the opposites of the following words by adding **dis** or **un** at the beginning.

lock   *unlock*   wise   *unwise*

obey   *disobey*   safe   *unsafe*

appear   *disappear*

trust   *distrust*

Underline the opposite of the word on the left.

74   **give**   lend   <u>take</u>   spend   have

75   **sink**   kitchen   drown   <u>rise</u>   lower

76   **finish**   end   find   dish   <u>start</u>

77   **junior**   <u>senior</u>   school   child   boy

78   **wild**   animal   fierce   <u>tame</u>   zoo

79–82   Underline the words which should start with a capital letter.

<u>matthew</u> and his mother went into the <u>countdown supermarket</u> to buy a packet of <u>chockomix</u>.

The names of some objects are shortened in everyday speech. What are the full names of the following?

83 photo   photograph   84 phone   telephone

85 exam   examination   86 T.V.   television

In each line there are two words which can be abbreviated.
Example: I am going to school. The **I am** can be written **I'm**.

87 We thought we would go to Chester.   we'd

88 "What I have got I intend to keep."   I've

89 I wonder what he will do when he starts work.   he'll

90 "It does not make sense to me," said Miss Jones.   doesn't

91 "Will the person who is making that noise stand up!"   who's

92 "Look! They have escaped at last."   They've

93 He will not stop teasing me.   won't

94 We are going to arrest that man.   We're

Here are some more pairs of words. Can you fit them into the sentences?

hand and foot   fits and starts   slow and sure   bits and pieces
sixes and sevens   ways and means

95 She took all her   bits and pieces   and went to London.

96 They found the   ways and means   to raise the money.

97 The old lady never went out. She seemed to be
bound   hand and foot   to her work.

98 After the burglars had left the room it was all at   sixes and sevens

99 Anna could have done better. She only worked by   fits and starts

100 Tom worked well as he was   slow and sure

46

Underline the right answers.

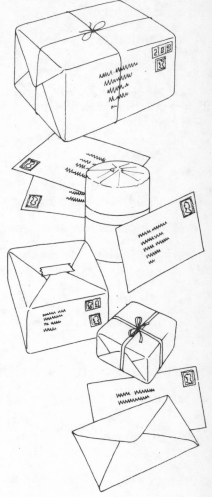

This is the Night Mail crossing the Border,
Bringing the cheque and the postal order.

Letters for the rich, letters for the poor,
The shop at the corner, the girl next door.

Pulling up Beattock, a steady climb:
The gradient's against her, but she's on time.

Past cotton-grass and moorland boulder,
Shovelling white steam over her shoulder,

Snorting noisily, she passes
Silent miles of wind-bent grasses.

Birds turn their heads as she approaches,
Stare from bushes at her blank-faced coaches.

Sheep-dogs cannot turn her course;
They slumber on with paws across.

In the farm she passes no one wakes,
But a jug in a bedroom gently shakes.

Dawn freshens. Her climb is done.
Down towards Glasgow she descends,
Towards the steam tugs yelping down a glade of cranes,
Towards the fields of apparatus, the furnaces
Set on the dark plain like gigantic chessmen.
All Scotland waits for her:
In dark glens, beside pale-green lochs,
Men long for news.

The Night Mail by W. H. Auden

1 Beattock is (a town, <u>a hill</u>, a shop)

2 Why don't the people at the farm wake up? (They don't hear the train, they are too far away, <u>they are used to the train</u>)

3 The jug shakes because (someone is using it, <u>the train makes it vibrate</u>, it is broken)

4 Does the train go up or down into Glasgow? (Up, <u>down</u>)

5 It reaches Glasgow in (the night, the day, <u>the dawn</u>, the evening)

6 Birds turn their heads (<u>to see what is making the noise</u>, because they are nervous, because they have stiff necks)

7 "She's on time" means (she has an alarm, <u>she is not late</u>, she has time to wake up)

8 "Turn her course" means (stop her, send her back again, <u>make her go another way</u>)

9 Which pronoun is used to describe the train? (<u>She</u>, it, they, he)

10 "Blank-faced coaches" are (<u>ones with no lights</u>, ones painted black, ones with black curtains)

11 "Gradient" is (grain, <u>slope</u>, weight, height)

12 "The Border" is (<u>a division</u>, an edging, a boulder)

Underline the word which rhymes with the one on the left.

13 **haze**   tease   <u>praise</u>   face   grace   waist

14 **foul**   soul   hole   bowl   <u>howl</u>   hen

15 **bite**   wit   hit   fit   lit   <u>sight</u>

16 **comb**   come   hum   <u>home</u>   brush   tomb

17 **wise**   <u>prize</u>   lost   mice   piece   was

Write a word which means the same as the word in heavy type.

18 The house had been **vacant** for some time.   empty

19 It was **suspended** from the ceiling.   hung

20 The girl was very **conceited**.   vain/proud

21 Michael had **completed** his work.   finished

22 He treated the horse very **brutally**.   cruelly

23 She **comprehended** what the man said.   understood

Give the feminine of:

24 gander ......goose......   25 prince ......princess......

26 uncle ......aunt......   27 landlord ......landlady......

28 manager ......manageress......   29 drake ......duck......

Write one word to complete each sentence.

30 Eye is to seeing as ear is to ......hearing......

31 Cuckoo is to bird as cat is to ......animal......

32 Sugar is to grocer as meat is to ......butcher......

33 Egg is to Easter as mince pie is to ......Christmas......

34 Fin is to fish as wing is to ......bird......

Complete the following sentences with a word linked with the word on the left.

35 good   Sally was the ......best...... writer in the class.

36 length   Tim has a ......longer...... stick than Kim.

37 fast   I can go ......faster...... than you.

38 bad   Miss Smith told Tara that her work was the ......worst...... in the class.

39 more   Anna had collected the ......most...... pictures.

Complete the following sentences, using the words listed below.

between   since   although   under   until   off   behind

40 ......Although...... I waved to her, she didn't see me.

41 ......Since...... I have been at this school I have learned to swim.

42 I cannot reach my books ......until...... you have moved that parcel.

43 There is a wall ......between...... the two gardens.

44 You must always sweep ......under...... the mats.

45 The little girl ran ......off...... the path.

46 The boy walked ......behind...... the cart.

49

Underline the word which does not fit in with the others.

47   thimble   needle   pin   <u>plate</u>   scissors

48   mound   <u>saucer</u>   hill   hillock   mountain

49   month   day   <u>May</u>   week   year

50   happy   merry   glad   pleased   <u>cross</u>

51   <u>rubber</u>   candle   light   torch   flame

52   fry   <u>beat</u>   heat   cook   boil

53   chair   bench   <u>table</u>   seat   settee

Underline the correct word or words in the brackets.

54   To exhibit is to (grow, <u>display</u>, exit, linger)

55   To invert means to (<u>reverse</u>, dress, interfere, climb)

56   To resemble is (to murmur, to resign, <u>to be like.</u> to assemble)

57   To surrender is (to suggest, to take, to come, <u>to yield)</u>

58   To maintain is (to climb, to master, <u>to keep,</u> to lose)

Choose a word from the list on the right to fill each space. The idea is to make a new, long word.
Example: snow drop snowdrop

59 tea spoon	60 cup board	coat	father
61 pen knife	62 grand father	paste	table
63 pillow case	64 over coat	knife	spoon
65 tooth paste	66 time table	board	case

Underline the word which does not fit in with the other words in the line.

67   cup   saucer   <u>cupboard</u>   dish   plate

68   green   blue   pink   <u>cloud</u>   red

69   robin   <u>lion</u>   thrush   sparrow   wren

70   snow   ice   hail   frost   <u>house</u>

71   <u>sing</u>   walk   jump   run   kick

72   Tom   Dick   <u>Jane</u>   Harry   Bill

Complete each sentence with one of the following words.

      sheet   feather   punch   hills   rock   cucumber

73   She was as pleased as ....*punch*.... when she passed her exam.

74   The book looked as old as the ....*hills*....

75   Even though it was a competition she was as cool as a ....*cucumber*....

76   Dad said that the wall was as steady as a ....*rock*....

77   When Keith got up he looked as white as a ....*sheet*....

78   The baby was as light as a ....*feather*....

Form adjectives linked with the words on the left.

79   sun   All the children liked the ....*sunny*.... classroom.

80   value   They had a ....*valuable*.... clock in the hall

81   wood   The ....*wooden*.... spoon was used for cake-making.

82   gold   They made a ....*golden*.... crown for the King.

83   beauty   The ....*beautiful*.... lady presented the prizes.

84   move   They went up on the ....*moving*.... staircase.

REQUIRED IMMEDIATELY
A boy or girl to deliver newspapers.
Hours 6.30 a.m. to 8 a.m. Mondays to Saturdays.
Wages £2 per day. It would be an advantage
if the applicant had a bicycle.
Write to Mr. Jones, Newsagent,
Pensby Road, Moreton.

85–90   Underline the statements that are correct.

The boy or girl must have a bicycle.
<u>He/She would be needed six days a week.</u>
<u>Mr. Jones wants a newsboy or girl quickly.</u>
There is no hurry to reply.
The boy/girl would get paid £4 a week.
<u>He/She would work nine hours a week.</u>

The boy/girl must go to see Mr. Jones.

Mr. Jones doesn't mind if he employs a girl or a boy.

The pay would be £12 a week.

It would be a help if the girl/boy had a bicycle.

On Monday icy rains poured down
and flooded drains all over town.
Tuesday's gales bashed elm and ash;
dead branches came down with a crash.
On Wednesday bursts of hail and sleet,
no-one walked along the street.
Thursday stood out clear and calm
but the sun was paler than my arm.
Friday's frost that bit your ears
was cold enough to freeze your tears.
Saturday's sky was ghostly grey;
we smashed ice on the lake today.
Christmas Eve was Sunday ... and
snow fell and fell across the land.

A Week of Winter Weather Wes Magee

91–92 On which days was it frosty?   Friday and Saturday

93–94 It snowed on Sunday . It rained on Monday .

95–96 It was very windy on Tuesday . When was there flooding? Monday

97–98 It hailed on Wednesday . Christmas Day was on Monday .

99 People stayed indoors on Wednesday .

100 We are told that there was no wind on Thursday .

Paper 11

Underline the right answers.

There is an old legend about Delhi (the capital of India). Long ago an old Hindu king was hammering a large iron nail into the earth, and as he swung with all his might the tip of the nail struck the head of the snake-god who supports the world on his coiled body. The king trembled at the thought of the snake-god's anger – would he bring fire and plague to his subjects, or even destroy the world? He ordered all his subjects to offer prayers and sacrifices to placate the snake-god. Several months passed and when the god's anger was soothed he told the king that he wouldn't punish him, but he said that on that spot there would always be war and unrest. The iron nail in this fable is supposed to be the Iron Pillar which today stands in the courtyard of a tower built about six hundred years ago. There is another legend which says that if you stand with your back to this pillar and can stretch your arms behind you round the pillar all your wishes will come true. I have watched many people try to do this but no one has had arms long enough to get more than half way round the pillar!

1 A legend is (something that happened a long time ago, something that happened in Bible times, a story, a true story)

2 "With all his might" means that (he used all his strength, he swung round, he fell over)

3 "Coiled" means (made of rope, curled round and round, put in a basket)

4–6 The king was frightened that the god would
(bring war, <u>destroy the earth, make people dreadfully ill,</u> flood
the earth, <u>cause terrible fires)</u>

7 To "placate" means (to put in place, to punish, <u>to please)</u>

8 The king's subjects were (words, <u>people,</u> thoughts, towns)

9–10 The king told his people (<u>to say prayers,</u> to tremble,
<u>to make sacrifices,</u> to fight)

11 Did the god punish the king and his people?
(Yes, no, I don't know, <u>yes, in a way they did not expect)</u>

12 Nowadays, do people find it easy to put their arms round the pillar?
(Yes, <u>no,</u> I don't know)

What jobs do these people have? Underline the most suitable word under each description.

13 He has a tanned, freckled face. He is wearing an old jacket and warm, heavy trousers which are stuck into green wellies; these are caked with mud. He carries a stick.
He is a   doctor,   <u>farmer,</u>   office worker,   steeplejack

14 He wears a pin-striped suit, a white shirt and a grey tie. His shoes are brightly polished, and he carries a briefcase.
He is a   bus-driver,   a fisherman,   a soldier,   <u>a solicitor</u>

15 She wears a crisp, white overall, and a stethoscope.
She is a   <u>doctor,</u>   groom,   taxi-driver,   builder

16 He wears old trousers, a tee-shirt, a helmet and protective shoes.
He is a   <u>builder,</u>   typist,   cobbler,   golf caddie

Underline one word in the brackets which is connected with the words on the left.

17 shoe   boot   sandal   (dress   <u>slipper</u>   hat   tea)

18 haddock   sole   cod   (ear-ring   match   hair   <u>herring)</u>

19 head   arm   leg   (glove   coat   sock   <u>foot)</u>

20 coach   car   train   (coat   <u>bus</u>   wait   run)

21 turnip   swede   potato   (garden   fruit   <u>carrot</u>   winter)

22 cup   glass   mug   (<u>beaker</u>   bread   water   china)

Write the opposite of the word in heavy type.

23 One puppy is **asleep**, but the other is ....awake........

24 This material is **coarse**, but yours is ....fine........

25 It is **dangerous** to swim here but over there it is ....safe........

26 David is **generous** but his brother is ....mean........

27 "Don't **frown**! You look much nicer when you ....smile........ "

Choose the most suitable word from the column on the right to fill each space.

28 The ....beat........ of a drum   tick

29 The ....jingle........ of coins   chattering

30 The ....chattering........ of monkeys   jingle

31 The ....crack........ of a whip   crack

32 The ....tick........ of a clock   beat

Choose one of the adverbs listed on the right to complete each sentence.

33 She acted ....quickly........ in the emergency.   generously

34 They waited ....anxiously........ at the hospital.   desperately

35 The prisoner fought ....desperately........ for his life. loudly

36 The postman knocked ....loudly........ on the door.   quickly

37 The farmer rose ....early........ in the morning.   anxiously

38 The lady gave ....generously........ to the collection. early

Underline the correct word in the brackets.

39 Uncle Martin is (learning, <u>teaching</u>) me to ride my bicycle.

40 Though Steven ran to the station he (<u>missed</u>, mist) his train.

41 Nobody has (never, <u>ever</u>) jumped that height before.

42 Anybody (<u>is</u>, are) allowed to go in.

43 The girl hasn't (nothing, <u>anything</u>) to do.

44 Both the boys (was, <u>were</u>) fighting.

Arrange the following words in dictionary order.

stilts   ship   seven   stick   shave   shape

45 (1) ....seven.......   **46** (2) ....shape.......   **47** (3) ....shave.......

48 (4) ....ship.......   **49** (5) ....stick.......   **50** (6) ....stilts.......

Write one word which means the same as the words in heavy type.

51 The man was **on time** for his appointment.   punctual

52 As we were in a hurry we **kept out of the way of** the crowds.   avoided

53 Justin's writing was poor, but now it is **getting better**.   improving

54 The **well-known** film star was surrounded by crowds of people.   famous

Underline one word in each line which does not agree with the rest.

55 hold   maintain   keep   <u>destroy</u>   retain

56 beautiful   <u>nasty</u>   lovely   pretty   handsome

57 <u>happy</u>   unwell   sick   ill   unhealthy

58 write   draw   scribble   paint   <u>kick</u>

59 wall   barrier   <u>house</u>   fence   hedge

60 gigantic   enormous   big   <u>tiny</u>   large

Look at these pairs of words. If they are alike in meaning write an A. If they are opposite write an O.

61 injure   harm   A

62 girl   boy   O

63 praise   blame   O

64 value   worth   A

65 entire   part   O

66 choose   select   A

67 silent   speechless   A

68 even   odd   O

Underline the word which has an opposite meaning to the word on the left.

69	**noise**	talk	shout	silence
70	**loose**	lose	soft	cover	tight
71	**sweet**	toffee	drop	sour	sugar
72	**some**	lots	none	more
73	**tall**	high	big	short

Make adjectives linked with the words on the left.

74 music   We had a .....musical..... evening at school last week.

75 nation   The dancers wore .....national..... costumes.

76 centre   We went to the .....central..... car park.

77 fashion   The model wore a very .....fashionable..... dress.

78 colour   Her coat was very .....colourful.....

79 misery   He felt .....miserable..... at home by himself.

Instead of writing **the towns of Africa** you could write **African towns**.
Do the same below.

80 The people of Wales are the .....Welsh..... people.

81 The rivers of Germany are .....German..... rivers.

82 The castles of Spain are .....Spanish..... castles.

83 The lakes of Ireland are .....Irish..... lakes.

84 The people of the West Indies are the .....West Indian..... people.

85 The cooking of Pakistan is .....Pakistani..... cooking.

In each line two words are abbreviated. Write them in full in the spaces.

86 They'll have to hurry up.   .....They will.....

87 He can't remember it now.   .....can not.....

88 She wants to know if you're going.   .....you are.....

89 He's only got one pair of shoes.   .....He has.....

90 Let's go to the disco.   .....Let us.....

91–100 In this poem, ten words are left out. See if you can fill them in.

Oh, I wish I'd looked ....after.... me teeth,

And spotted the perils beneath,

All the toffees I ....chewed....

And the sweet, sticky food,

....Oh...., I wish I'd looked after ....me.... teeth.

I wish I'd been ....that.... much more willin'

When I ....had.... more tooth there ....than.... fillin'

....To.... pass up gobstoppers

From respect ....for.... me choppers,

And to buy ....something.... else with me shillin'.

Pam Ayres

58

Paper 12

Underline the right answers.

First came ten soldiers carrying clubs; these were all shaped like the three gardeners, oblong and flat, with their hands and feet at the corners: next the ten courtiers; these were ornamented all over with diamonds, and walked two and two, as the soldiers did. After these came the royal children; there were ten of them, and the little dears came jumping merrily along hand in hand, in couples; they were all ornamented with hearts. Next came the guests, mostly Kings and Queens, and among them Alice recognised the White Rabbit: it was talking in a hurried, nervous manner, smiling at everything that was said, and went by without noticing her. Then followed the Knave of Hearts, carrying the King's crown on a crimson velvet cushion; and, last of all this grand procession, came The King and Queen of Hearts.

From *Alice in Wonderland* by Lewis Carroll

1   Who led the procession? (The gardeners, the soldiers, the White Rabbit)

2   Who were jumping merrily along hand in hand?
    (The royal children, the King and Queen, rabbits)

3   Which guest did Alice recognise?
    (The gardener, the White Rabbit, the Knave of Hearts)

4   Who were ornamented all over with diamonds?
    (The soldiers, the courtiers, the King and Queen of Hearts)

5   Who was carrying the King's crown?
    (Alice, the Knave of Hearts, the White Rabbit)

6   Who were ornamented with hearts?
    (The guests, the courtiers, the royal children)

7–8 Who were the most important people in the procession?
    (Alice, the King of Hearts, the White Rabbit, the Queen of Hearts)

9   How many royal children were there? (Two, I don't know, ten)

10   Who didn't notice Alice?
(The soldiers, the courtiers, <u>the White Rabbit,</u> the gardeners)

11   What were the soldiers carrying? (Diamonds, hearts, spades, <u>clubs</u>)

12   Which group was fourth in the procession?
(The soldiers, <u>the guests,</u> the royal children, the gardeners)

Write one word which has the same meaning as the words in heavy type.

13   Marilyn has learnt to skate **with ease**.   easily

14   We are **not allowed** to run on the grass.   forbidden

15   The naughty boy **was sorry for** what he had done.   regretted

16   At one o'clock I feel **the need for food**.   hungry

Some words sound the same but are spelled differently. Can you underline the right one in the brackets?

17   They set up their deck-chairs on the (<u>beach</u>, beech)

18   There is a (beach, <u>beech</u>) tree in the garden.

19   (<u>Our,</u> hour) television is broken.

20   It takes me one (our, <u>hour</u>) to get to school.

21   Sam (<u>led</u>, lead) the way to the toy counter.

22   (Led, <u>lead</u>) is a metal.

Underline the correct word inside the brackets.

23   They have (sang, <u>sung</u>, singed) in the choir.

24   We have (<u>run</u>, ran, runned) all the way.

25   He has (fell, fall, <u>fallen</u>) down the steps.

26   She was (laying, <u>lying</u>, laid) on the bed.

27   He had (ate, <u>eaten</u>, ate) all the apples.

28   We have (spoke, speak, <u>spoken</u>) to her about it.

Underline the word which best describes the word on the left.

29 **lesson**   famous   <u>interesting</u>   large   ready

30 **train**   good   fare   fair   <u>express</u>

31	**climate**	lazy	small	<u>warm</u>	late
32	**colour**	<u>bright</u>	wet	painted	cloudy
33	**water**	wet	dry	dusty	<u>hot</u>
34	**fireman**	cold	<u>brave</u>	dark	stormy

Choose a word from the list on the right to fill each space, making a new, longer word.

35	tooth <u>ache</u>	36	flower <u>pot</u>	yard	ball
37	foot <u>ball</u>	38	book <u>case</u>	tray	ache
39	church <u>yard</u>	40	ash <u>tray</u>	case	pot

Underline the word which is the same part of speech as the word on the left.

41	**me**	girl	boy	am	fat	<u>them</u>
42	**quickly**	lean	<u>slowly</u>	she	speed	was
43	**lovely**	girl	she	is	how	<u>warm</u>
44	**ate**	food	<u>drank</u>	man	he	bread
45	**teacher**	<u>baby</u>	he	taught	me	us
46	**and**	hand	more	me	<u>but</u>	add

Underline the word which rhymes with the word on the left.

47	**ewe**	were	sew	<u>few</u>	throw
48	**word**	lord	board	sword	<u>heard</u>
49	**sole**	<u>foal</u>	alone	gone	sell
50	**chair**	gear	<u>mare</u>	seat	year
51	**pear**	dear	far	jar	<u>dare</u>

Underline the word which has an opposite meaning to the word on the left.

52	**narrow**	long	short	<u>wide</u>	near
53	**finish**	conclude	complain	end	<u>start</u>
54	**shallow**	<u>deep</u>	low	under	allow

55	**hinder**	stop	<u>help</u>	back	under
56	**gentle**	good	kind	<u>rough</u>	man
57	**go**	went	back	forward	<u>come</u>
58	**borrow**	spend	take	<u>lend</u>	sorrow

Underline the word which means the same as the word on the left.

59	**halt**	go	<u>stop</u>	come	red
60	**distress**	mistress	distant	<u>misery</u>	far
61	**timid**	<u>shy</u>	proud	sad	good
62	**guard**	train	hard	govern	<u>protect</u>
63	**observe**	desert	<u>watch</u>	leave	object
64	**rich**	poor	happy	<u>wealthy</u>	sad

Form nouns linked with the words on the left.

65 collect Mark was very proud of his stamp <u>collection</u>

66 feed They put the <u>food</u> in the fridge.

67 know The man's <u>knowledge</u> of sport was remarkable.

68 drive James wanted to be a racing <u>driver</u>

69 warm The <u>warmth</u> from the fire made him sleepy.

70 see The <u>sight</u> of the hills filled me with happiness.

71–80 Fill in the missing letters.

The old house stands at the c<u>orne</u>r of the road.
It is almost c<u>overe</u>d with ivy and there is
a b<u>eauti</u>ful garden all round it. Part of
the house is said to be four h<u>undre</u>d years
old. The c<u>urtai</u>ns at the large windows are
made of heavy silk. There are fo<u>rt</u>y rooms in the
house but they are not all used. The furn<u>iture</u>
is old too, and most of it is very val<u>uable</u>.
Queen Elizabeth I is sup<u>pos</u>ed to have slept in
one of the bedrooms but no one can be s<u>ure</u> that
this is true.

62

Underline two words in each line which have something in common with the word on the left.

81–82	**clock**	face	legs	ankles	hands	feet
83–84	**door**	book	handle	lesson	hinge	floor
85–86	**chair**	face	legs	hands	seat	top
87–88	**piano**	keys	locks	wheels	station	pedals

Every sixth word has been left out of this poem. Can you fill them in?

89–96

All this sea

And only ...me....

To watch it crawl

With ...rise... and fall,

Over the sand

Where. now I stand,

At break ....of..... day

A castaway.

At dead .....of..... night

And no starlight

I _hear_ it roar

Towards the shore,

...And... full of tears

I stop .....my.... ears

I want a friend

Exile to end

97–100   Underline the adjectives in the following passage:

Cinderella slept in a cold garret, on a wretched, straw bed, while her

step-sisters lay in fine rooms.

Total marks

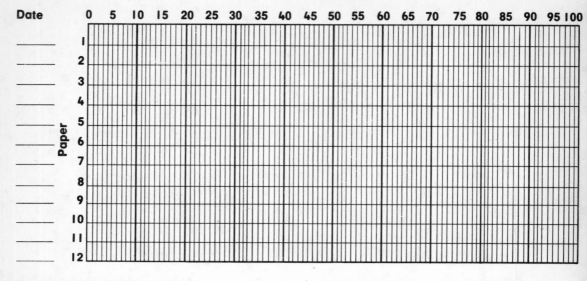

Date

Paper

Thomas Nelson and Sons Ltd
Nelson House Mayfield Road
Walton-on-Thames Surrey
KT12 5PL UK

© **J M Bond 1965, 1983, 1988, 1994**

First published 1965
Revised edition 1983
Reprinted 1987, 1988
This fully revised edition 1994

I(T)P Thomas Nelson is an International
       Thomson Publishing Company

I(T)P is used under licence

Pupil's book ISBN 0-17-424525-4
              NPN 9
Answer book ISBN 0-17-424526-2
             NPN 9 8 7

By the same author
First, Second, Third, Fourth and Further
Fourth Year Assessment Papers in Mathematics

First, Second, Third, Fourth and Further
Fourth Year Assessment Papers in English

First, Second, Third, Fourth and Further
Fourth Year Assessment Papers in Reasoning

Printed in Croatia.

Poems and extracts reproduced by kind permission of

Dolphin Concert Productions Ltd: Extract from **Oh I
wish I'd looked after me teeth** by Pam Ayres (Paper 1
Faber & Faber Ltd: **The Night Mail** from *Collected
poems* by W H Auden (Paper 10) and **Kenneth**
from *The Book of Comic Verse* by Wendy Cope
(Paper 2)
Oxford University Press; **Four o'clock** from
Tomorrow is my Love by Hal Summers
© Hal Summers 1978 (Paper 3)
Mrs A M Walsh: **Journey Home** from *The
Roundabout by the Sea* by John Walsh (Paper 6)
Cambridge University Press: **The School Year** and
A Week of Winter Weather by Wes Magee
(Papers 4 and 10)
George Allen & Unwin: Extract from *The Hobbit*
by J R R Tolkien (Paper 5)
William Heinemann Ltd: Extract from
101 Dalmations by Dodie Smith (Paper 7)

The publishers have made every attempt to trace
copyright holders of reprinted material, and
apologise for any errors or omissions.